McFadyen, Warwick
The Centre of Zero
ISBN 978-0-6458923-4-5

Published by McFadyen Media
PO Box 19 Gisborne Victoria 3437
©2024 Warwick McFadyen
Design and production: PB Publishing

Copyright resides with the author. The moral rights of the author have been asserted.
Photographs: Warwick McFadyen

Some of the poems in this book have appeared previously in the author's books The Ocean and 21 + 4.

 A catalogue record for this book is available from the National Library of Australia

WARWICK McFADYEN

The Centre of Zero

Poems 2019 – 2024

To Pip and Grace
and, forever gone,
and forever within,
Hamish.

These poems are the tidal charts from the past
five years. If there is an overlap within them and
to another, that's the waves coming up against
each other, and the currents rising and falling. In
the wash of life and loss, there is a centre that
can hold. It is love.

CONTENTS

WATER — 1
- Flow — 2
- The Rockpool — 3
- The Unbreaking Wave — 4
- The Wake — 5
- River — 6
- The Ledge — 7
- The Swimmer — 8
- To the Ocean — 9
- Bridge — 10
- The Sea and the Dream — 11
- Time and Blood — 12

LIGHT — 13
- Intimations — 14
- Winter is Upon the Earth — 16
- The Leaving (when spring comes) — 17
- The Light that Travels — 19
- Nightfall — 20
- On Seeing — 21
- Autumn Twilight (For Peter) — 22
- Glint — 23
- All These Things — 25
- Threads of Light — 26

EARTH — 27
- Into the Grain — 28
- Another Graveyard — 29
- The Rose Within — 31
- The Plaque — 32
- Compass — 34
- Map — 36
- A Graveyard on Anzac Day — 39

Early Morning	40
The Harvest	41
Easter Sunday	42
The Weight	43
Oak and Acorn	44

VOICES — 45

The Wait (Father to Son)	46
The Door	47
The Second Christmas	48
So It Goes	50
Listen	51
Two Zeroes	52
Life in a Word	54
Deeper	55
Gift	56
Still Life	57

TIME — 58

The Hours	59
Incantation	60
Call/Response	62
Sleep/Awake	63
If, 2023	64
Artificial Intelligence/It could be Anyone	66
An Afternoon Storm in the New Year	67
Hand and Glove	68
The October Poem	69
Span	71
Stone and Star	72
The Air Moves	73
The Glass	74
True North	75
The Centre of Zero	76
AFTERWORD	77

The Centre of Zero

WATER

Flow

Empty this into my heart —
the sky, the infinite surface,
let me feel when I look within
that I am looking out as well.

Empty this into my heart —
the wash and whorl of the sea
let me feel the tide's pull and push
of moonlight and shadow.

Empty this into my heart —
the light of distant stars
that I might hold close the wisp
of time that I can say is only mine.

Empty this into my heart —
the whisper of wind on worn stone
that I can listen, and return it
in a voice, never emptying.

The Rockpool

Where sea meets shore
there is a hollow
in the rock that cradles
the ocean's leaving.

In its shallows,
like a memory,
the wash of the depths
is briefly held.

For storms may visit
the rough flush
of wilding waves
upon its core

And take the thing
itself but, in the
taking, redeem
anew a part of itself.
Becalmed, silent,
kissed by the waves
of the sun, it offers
reflection like a prayer.

Ocean and pool
coalesce, from
horizon's edge
to hollow in rock.

In the receding is the return.

The Unbreaking Wave

Not as a flower holds light,
but as the wave
that never breaks
the sky holds infinity.

Not as we hold time
nestling in flesh and bone,
but as the sigh of the stars,
the sky holds infinity.

Not as a promise to us,
but as the mirror
that reflects upon itself,
the sky holds infinity.

The sky holds infinity,
not for our purpose,
but we carry this:
for each pin of light

that falls to earth
we transform
the untouchable
into the touched.

A small thread
of luminescence
we go, a flower cast
upon the wave.

The Wake

The surface breaks and in the parting
lines of ripples slip away.
They crest then fade into the fold
that swirls and sleeps under the spray.

This is the lapping of each moment
from rock of cradle to silent grave,
this is the voice that no longer travels
but for what it left and what it gave.

This is the widening wake, carrying
the echo and call of a life now past
to my shore-bound days. The water
runs through my hands. I hold it fast.

River

I am walking on the river bed
for the river no longer flows.
Now it feels the wind and sun
and falling moonlight's glow.

Now under the dry surface it holds
onto the thing it once had been;
the rhythms, pools and stillness,
all to the world unseen.

This is the land of droughts and flooding
rains. This is the landscape passing
within, of ripple and swirl
as one, then vanishing.

Each life is a river.

The Ledge

I watch the surfers
take off
over the ledge
fall into the wave
breaking
over their shoulder.
I can see
the line of ocean
drawing itself
to the waiting shore,
the symmetry of sky
merging into
the aqua music,
the glissando
of swell
become surf
then surfer.

In that moment
my eyes fill
with the light
that turns
on the tide.
A surfer takes off
over the ledge,
for joy,
for dear life.

The Swimmer

In early light I stroke
the surface of the
sea-gathered pool,
each ripple I send
to the waiting rim
falls back on itself
and cannot ascend
over and beyond
the path I swim.

But here I know
in the water calm
and in the tow
of my path, in
the glide of my arm,
in my drawing of breath
love is both ebb and flow
of ocean and pool;
in its currents there, I go.

To the Ocean

In the shallows of the shoreline,
I bend to the water and gather the sea.
It slips through my hands from its time
of leaving. I cannot hold it close to me.

On the worn path in the forest,
I walk with the sun and gather the light.
It brushes my skin, and then falls
away. I cannot keep it within my sight.

And yet these moments are landscape;
my horizons, atlas of flickering line.
On sand, still wet, I write a life
in one letter, hold it forever with mine.

This is reflex of emotion.
This is the tide running.
This is the ocean.

Bridge

A bridge requires two sides
and a gulf in between,
its reason for being
there is at times unseen.

The space for the crossing
may be water or stone,
it may be held words that
wait to not be alone.

It may be a river
of tears everflowing,
it may be the dried bed
now with weeds agrowing.

The bridge is the hand you
open to grasp another's
to feel the rise and fall
of what love discovers.

The Sea and the Dream

The river braids through
shoals of half-light
on its way to the sea.

A swimmer head down
stroke after stroke
breath after breath to be

At one with the flow
struggles free of
the aeolian tide

To feel the currents
course to deeper
waters on the inside

of the dark circle
that is the edge
of each rotating wheel

that turns, and then once
turned, fades and the
dream is no longer real.

Time and Blood

Pools, rivers, streams and dams
the stop start flow of cells,
closed circuit rhythm cams
to touch where the heart dwells

to give us blood red time
that we think we will know
a fixed reason and rhyme.
But we only follow

the sun rising and night
falling; that in holding
to a star's promised light
is darkness enfolding.

Breathe then with undimmed eyes
while you can, catch the air
that whispers, roars and sighs,
swim the tide as a prayer.

LIGHT

Intimations

Through shade of tree
and light of sun
  the path leads,

A rustle of meditation
whispers, There will always
                be time.

There
    will
        not
            be
                time
                    sighs
                        a
                          cloud.

Under heavens that spark,
in the days that flicker
        in the scrape

of worlds against worlds
go I: incantation and
            inhalation.
Intimations wash over my eyes
like rolling waves breaking
                into foam.
Till human voices wake us,
and we drown.
No, it is not that.

But this: each voice is a
constellation, a flash of comets,
 and fixed stars

flaring and fading out
the breath rises, then dies,
 within the chambers

that we carry; our universe,
a sky bruised with hope;
 this is our love song.

And the path is a coil of the heart
that sings from the warmth
 of the sun.

We walk in the shade.

We walk in the light.

Winter is Upon the Earth

The light that bore summer
within it is fading
and reforming;
less of the sun,
more of the moon.
Like a tide going out
and returning,
ice-capped:
winter is upon us.

Residing within
the turning days
that move through
blood, flesh and bone.
At times, rising as a storm
carrying bruised clouds
or settling as a frozen pond
at the bottom of the still heart.
A guest that cannot be turned away.
The chill air slaps our senses awake;
we fold warmth into our hands,
blow on them to keep it alive.
In a darkened season, in this
pale light, we look for a path.

The Leaving
(When spring comes)

Oaks once slumbering
stretch their limbs
in the spring air,
the earth underfoot
pulses with
awakening life.

Light pours in,
where once
it glistened
on the rim
of frost-touched
mornings.

As if bent from a magnet's
attraction, the light now
casts shadows out
of silence and sways
not the rhythm
of the season but the heart.

Another anniversary blooms
unwanted, uncalled.
This is the untended garden
of tireless love and memory
where the young roots taunt:
we will never die,
for we have become the sap rising,
and the colours turning,
the veins of the new leaf,
and the leaf falling.

We have entered the bloodstream
and made the heart our home.

In the widening of the years,
in the turning of the seasons
the distance grows, we age
while zero remains zero.
This is the equation of loss.
This is the long leaving.

The Light that Travels

It was bin night – yellow and green
I placed them on the kerb
and, walking back to the house,
I looked up into the night sky
and tried to read the stars
left to right and back again;
a stream of centuries' light
had travelled to me in the blackness,
in the ordinary rituals. On bin night.
Thank you, I said, as quiet as star dust.

I knew my words could not rise
to the stars. They fell fading to earth
or were borne away on a swirl of air.
Yet they stayed with me; a pulse,
an echo in the heart's chamber.

The stars that night were not mine,
though I held their distance close;
scientists may give them names,
while we see what we dream them to be.
On bin night - yellow and green
I looked up into the night sky
and knew that even as one star died,
its light still travelled through
the emptiness and nestled
in my eyes, on bin night, until
I too would return to dust.

Nightfall

When the light
fades into the sky.
When the air
settles as a sigh.

When the stars
flick their switch.
When the moon
makes it pitch

to sleep, to sleep:
this is the time
for your dreams
to flow and rhyme

with the rhythm
of a beating heart
with the whisper,
make this start

knowing the wind
will rise,
and the dust will
enter your eyes.

This is the cycle
of nightfall:
before and after,
the sun will call.

On Seeing

For a few minutes
I stare at the points
of light, flaring
and blurring
into the blackness.
For a few minutes
I reach out and
run my fingers
over their life
and death.

For a few seconds
I allow myself
a smile to infinity,
drink the last dregs
of my coffee
And go out
into the day,
knowing those
13 billion years
will always be there.

Autumn Twilight
(For Peter)

The day was folding into night
as I walked the streets of my town.
The sky fading from blue to black
was slipping on quietude's gown.

Not a sound, but the call of birds
creased the air. I could not sing
their lullabies, for I knew
their melodies they did not bring

to me. The lights of homes began
to shine in the passing windows
as in the gathering dark
more stars would come into show.

For now, a crescent moon seemed
to hang by an invisible thread
alone but for one star near — not
to guide but to the heavens to wed

the light that is carried to us
with the light in our eyes -
that in this inhalation of day's
waning, we breathe a sky's

stillpoints of wonders
and become alchemists
of beauty, blessed to have
been both star and moon kissed.

Glint

The wash of the moon
dream-limned
from a million eyes
streamed in
and brushed
against my face.

Awakened, I asked,
What is it that
you came to visit?
The moon replied,
This is not a love song.
I've brought you this:

It's the dust
God shook off
his great coat
after he had stopped
arguing with
his younger self.

It's the particles
of worlds
that vanished
before time
had a face
recognisable.

It's the numbers
of the universe
broken up
by the tremor
of a bird's
beating wing.

It's the grain
that floats
among the stars
come to rest
as the glint and grit
in your eyes.

These things
are the fading
and the thrum,
the shadow
and the light of life.
Listen, see, speak.

All These Things

The wind wild and ragged,
the sky a splintered flag.
A voice that remains
in a pool of light
The stars each a shard,
the earth underfoot.
A voice that remains
in a pool of light
The river, raft of time,
each grain of sand a beach.
A voice that remains
in a pool of light.
The mist nestling soft,
the slumbering day.
A voice that remains
in a pool of light.
The whisper of a cloud,
the heartbeat travelling.
A voice that remains
in a pool of light.

Threads of Light

At the rising of the sun while
the morning still is sleeping
and the air carries the colours
of the day in its keeping

I stand at the water's edge and
let the tide softly sing me
its moon rhythm, ripple within,
hear the murmur of the sea

like a thread in the undertow
whispering against the night:
the grace notes of life are the stars,
forming into threads of light.

EARTH

Into the grain

This tree grows
from roots seen
and unseen.
Higher, wider
it rises
branching,
wilting,
blooming,
shearing.

Life and death
run in its veins;
rain and drought
seep into the fibres
that colour the grain
that shape its spine,
one to give, one to
take, both part of
creation's cycle.

This tree bends
in the high wind,
takes the gusts
and gales of storms
with the fall
of shadows and sun
across its leaf.
It carries the weather
in its arms.

But still the bough
can break,
the trunk can topple.
It has no shield
strong enough to stop
the snap of its roots
no matter how far
they reach
into the earth.

And yet, this tree grows

From the words
that form in a deep
well and rise to enter
in the grain of your life.
Love, always love.

Another Graveyard

I didn't mean to be among
the bones and ash
of the graveyard cradling
life gone and memory fixed.
The clouds pulled me, the sun
guided me, to flowers in vases,
to the worn edges of stone
and the dried tears of farewell.
Among the oaks and turned soil
settling into eternity,
headstones and plaques sigh
among themselves; each a life,
now folded into words and dates,
each an etching on the passing years,
while unmarked graves, of adult
and child, go unremarked.
Divided by path and patches of lawn
death has its order: by alphabet
and by boundaries of tribes
who believe they know
the contours of the darkness
after it falls. I sit in the sunlight
and shadows and know only this:
visitors all, we are borne on the breeze.

And are gone.

The Centre of Zero

The Rose Within

I didn't know till now
of the distance
in the petals of a rose.

It had always been beguiling,
the beauty and the thorn,
the touch and the nick.

Now the light settles in
its folds as if it has fallen
from the rim of the moon.

It washes against the colours
like the tide against rocks
leaves drops of itself in pools.

It has become the horizon
within that once reached
no longer exists.

It is the silence of a piano
when the keys once played
by the sun are now still.

It is the slant of the sky
deep in the opened bloom.
Infinity caught for a moment.

The plaque

Look, this is for you
here is your name
date of birth
date of death
the bookends
of your life
and then a few words
scooped from the sea
washing over us
to be forever
etched into brass
for the sun to kiss
the wind to brush
the rain to touch
the hand to stroke
the smile to bless
the sigh to cause
the heart to rise
and fall.

Look, here is the stone
in the ground
— the mark blood stilled
and blind to the world
that speaks in the silence
with the light of dawn,
with the drawing
of the dark
you were alive
and now are forever
among strangers
among your silent kind
on the edge

of a garden bed
ashes fed, tears watered
where birds peck the earth
where you, undisturbed,
sleep not — for that
is for the living —
but behind our eyes.

Look, here I sit
on a park bench
an arm's length
from you.
Eternity nuzzles
next to me,
a ribbon of sky
come to earth.
I turn to it,
saying, who knew
you could hold
three years
and today
at the same time.
The ribbon rustles
in the breeze.
But we know,
the graves and
plaques whisper.
We know.

Compass

To hold a compass in my palm
and watch the needle stay true
while winds sing a ragged psalm
O, wanderer, we thought you knew

Even to eyes cast northward bound
even to the southern bands
the lines of sight stay not ground
like time-weathered marks on your hands.

The direction to a life borne
is cloaked in shadow and light
the heartbeat of the hours drawn
into the wash of your life's flight.

But the compass, I tell the wind,
lives within and shapes the road.
It is the sky and soul twinned.
It is the seed, the harvest sowed.

From earth risen a rustling laughs:
the magnetic lines of their
own are not your guiding paths
but streams of us that course through air.

And still then the compass is held
for bones are not skeletal
when breath is life, and the weld
of heart and mind defines the call:

The eye of the needle is me
From north, south, east and the west
It is the sky, it is the sea,
the stillpoint to the wind's tempest.

Map

The world was on the wall
of the classroom.
Mercator was its name.
The earth pinned flat -
oval frames of creation
reference points -
was the span
of my child arms.

Meridians travelled
over bodies of
land and water
wrapping the globe,
like a gift,
in the certainties
of a mapmaker's
measurements.

I placed my fingers
on the places
where one day I said
I would go.
One day.
One day.
The lines were
a projection.

And then I was
in the world.
Each route I took,
each path I trod,
each breath,
was a mark on a map.

Straight lines
and circles
settled under the skin.

There the past resided,
going about its business.
Rising now
and again
to say you wouldn't be here
if you hadn't been there.
One day.
One day.
The lines were a projection

Of destination and departure,
an atlas of distance
the traveller takes
and does not;
of lands unexplored,
voices unheard,
whispers unmet,
touch unexplored,
eyes unopened.

On the Imago Mundi,
birds end not their flight,
the light is brighter
than sunrise and sunset;
darkness enfolds,
beasts roam
and dawn comes.
The lines were a projection.

This then is the map
within and
without you.
The lines on your face
and hands,
the words that rise
from valleys,
that skirt the sky
from mountains.

A Graveyard on Anzac Day

In Gisborne graveyard
the leaves are falling,
from acorn to oak,
the seasons are calling
to each of us, a leaf
in the breeze,
a whisper in time,
a tear to the seas.

In Gisborne graveyard
the soldier stands head
bowed, his body cast
forever to mark the dead.
On this Anzac Day, he is
among headstone and grave
a sentinel among the quiet
multitudes of the same dark wave.

In Gisborne graveyard
two women kneel to place
flowers by a plaque; they
embrace, lean in face to face.
One waters the roots
for a longer life, they must,
one supposes, while the other
brushes away the dust.

Early Morning

I walk the airs
Of early morning.
The song of magpie,
caw of crow
and cockatoo,
the burble of the creek
in its rushing
between the deeper
scouring when the current
slows and sound
bides its time,
these are the rhythms
playing on the sky,
a notation on the wind.
Into this a stillness
falls onto my skin.
I can feel its rub
as it seeps into
the bloodstream,
is carried into
the chambers
of the heart.
This is nature's valve
where silence and voice
become the pulse
of memory, and are
released into the day.
This is the soul's air
and grace.

The Harvest

It's the season of growing
and the paddocks are brown.

The colour of faith is undimmed,
yet the paddocks are brown.

It's the time of renewal
and the dams are all dry.

The call to trust is unshaken,
yet the dams are all dry.

It's the season of unfolding
and the earth it is cracked.

The heart is still full,
yet the earth it is cracked.

Easter Sunday

The bones of Christ were long gone
to dust, the ripples of the waves
said to me as I walked the shore.
And as I walked, my footprints
dissolved back into the sand,
just like time's work on the bones,
the waves whispered, the moon
and the tides could not be denied.
The sun was on the horizon,
just rising, carrying its distance
in the heartbeat of the day.
On this day death became a question
where was thy sting when ascension
transformed the white of the waves
to hands raised to the waiting sky?
But the bones of Christ were long gone,
returned to carbon, became the matter
of stars that shone into infinity.
And so I walked the shore, and felt the sun
on my skin, warming me, going deep,
deep into the wash of my bloodstream.

The Weight

Who knew that ashes would weigh the same
in your arms as when you held him as a baby.
You hold them close to your chest,
your heart breaking, this is not something

you were expecting, to be sent back 20 years
to the cradling of love, small soft body
against yours now an emptiness of sky
heavy on your breast.

Each breath is a word, spoken or unsaid,
but what can you say as you place him
in a snug shovel-dug hole in the earth
but keep warm, my beautiful boy.

We brush the plaque now sitting over him
with our fingers - a kiss goodbye of love.
We take a small jar of him home with us.
We have his smile, we say in tear-mist breath.

That night a light rain falls and I think of him
alone in the damp earth. You are not alone I say.
You are not alone.

Oak and Acorn

Do the oaks pray
for their children
on leaf buffeted and
cradled by wind and sun,
may you fall
on earth soft and damp,
may you be a song
and grow towards
the light, a voice strong?

Do the acorns pray
as they ripen
on leaf buffeted and
cradled by wind and sun
may we fall
in earth soft and damp
may we be a song
and grow towards
the light, a voice strong?

In the nature of
things, the wind,
sun and ground
sigh, oak and acorn
there is a tide
of fortune
golden and grey
ascending and
falling in every day.

May you both
in the whispering
and the roar,
pray the wind, sun
and ground,
know that in
the seasons turning
you are both one
to stars, returning.

VOICES

The Wait
(Father to son)

Here now
— coming.

Exchange
typed
of flesh
and blood.

Here now
— coming.
Call and
response
now ghost
words.

Here now
— coming.

The empty
screen,
the silence
of ash.

Here now
— coming.
Here now
— coming.

Every day he
walks
inhaling
the infinity
of the sky.
It's an exercise
of the mind:
If he keeps
walking,
maybe he'll run
into him.
Maybe he'll come
full circle,
before zero
became eternity.

Here now
— coming.

No more.
In the here
and now.

The Door

Once I could open this door
though I can see it still.

I could greet the eyes,
touch the skin.

Once I could open this door
and words would meet.

At beginning and end
the door knows only

that it opens, shuts,
silently stands.

Time was, was once time
that I could open this door

believing I had all the time
in my hands, in the world.

No one has all the time,
the hinge on the door

swings open, swings shut
without us, within us.

The Second Christmas

A crow caws
in a captured sky,
it rises and dives
in a flickering eye.

Its wings bring
the flutter of
a darkness deep —
but I am love

it says, though
of the hardest kind;
by the restless air my wings
to your heart bind.

I take your
breath in wisp and wave,
release it to the stars —
knowing none can save

the drawing
of more, for the flow
is a promise of memory
that will not slow.
I exist,
it says, because one does not.
I live within the space
of a caprice, a knot
that takes shape
without reasons
or order to the rhyme
of the fixed seasons.

A phoenix
I am not; I cannot give
rise to what has been lost
nor my birth forgive.

So It Goes

It's hard not to ask
looking up at the sky
in all of the vastness,
Where is the I?

Among the stars, planets
and moons, in the sigh
of our sleepless time,
there you are, they reply.

But I see not me,
no footprint, nor mark
of life's signature
in the spreading dark.

No echo of my voice
returns, and I fear
the words I speak
are but a falling tear.

So it goes, the wind
whispers, so it goes.
The biggest things
Are folded unto a rose.

Carry its beauty
and you carry the world;
and there you live,
your eyes unfurled.

Listen

Imagine the voices of the world
now silenced rising
from the earth,
like early morning mist,
wisps of calls, looking
for echoes before
burning off in the sun
and fading out.

Imagine the voice of one
falling, as if no longer
a feather on the wind,
but into the darkness
enfolding
that is the cradle
of stone and soil
and silence.

These passing notes,
this staff of souls,

this ascending
and descending,
this lightness,
this weight
of being human.
Listen.

Two Zeroes

From zero to zero
we span a little thread
vibrate to the sigh
and shout,
the wail and whisper,
kiss and caress.
We are the tremor
in the air that in the
moving is moved.

How can the sum
of it be zero
isn't the question.

The shadow
of our sway
will in time
seep into the
waiting sky,
become the fabric
we once looked
into, and
we
will
be
gone.

How can the sum
of it be zero
isn't the question.
Between two zeroes
was the touch
of the hand
against the clouds,
the trace of a name
in the echo of a
chain of voices,
in the space
between two zeroes.

Life in a Word

Each word to you
is a breath
I give in return,
as thanks, as prayer,
as the hand
outstretched to bring
silence close.

For time takes in
and takes out
the air that fills
the cupped voice.
And language born
of the wind
must follow its
rise and fall.

I give in return
each word to you.
And as I breathe
slant of light
and shadow
define the words
I give
in return
for you.

Deeper

How to mine the deeper meaning
I asked a magpie on the wing.
It trilled an answer air on air
that in its notes I could not sing.

How to mine the deeper meaning
I asked the lapping of the wave.
It rose and broke upon the shore,
the ebb and flow was all it gave.

How to mine the deeper meaning
I asked the weathered rustling leaf.
It bowed and bent with sighing breeze,
Time is a thief, time is a thief.

How to mine the deeper meaning
I asked the stars overhead.
They said when our light touches you
know in the parting are the dead.

How to mine the deeper meaning
I asked the rain and earth and stream.
They replied, in the life of one
dwells another. Love is the seam.

Gift

Not every word is a poem,
not every sound is a song.
Undo the knot, said the pair,
in our dreams you can be strong.

This is the gift, listen —
when the gales of night
rage and the stars fold
to black — for the light

That comes in voices
as the threads that bind
so we speak, and sing
This is love in kind.

For what price is paid
if what is spoken
only seeks to see
hands and tongues broken.

Not every word is a stone,
not every sound is a click.
So rang out the poem and song:
in our dreams you can be strong.

Still Life

Is the guitar silent if hands
upon the strings do not play?
Are violin and harp untouched
mere wire and wood at bay?

Is the piano mute when fingers
do not press upon the keys?
Is the flute without a breath
the sky without a breeze?

On the edges of the wild surf,
in the shadows of night falling,
the notes within an instrument
are waiting for their calling.

Is a voice not heard silence?
In its waiting, so life becomes.
The resting heart begins to stir,
a string vibrates, the air thrums.

We are the players and the played.

TIME

The Hours

I tried to hold the hours in my hand
but I couldn't make a fist of it.

And yet I wait for light of sun,
crest of moon to fall into its grasp

and coalesce as prayer that day's
shadow will not lengthen as

time demands it must. In the end,
everything becomes nothing to it.

But between those two points
the open hand tries to keep close

a distance further than star and moon.
This is loss for love immeasurable.

This is the soul's timepiece:
My heart knows this my heart.

Incantation

The jewels you hold close
are not the ones you wear.
The light in your eyes
is not the glow of gems.
The sound of your voice
is not the cut of stone.
The touch of your hand
is not the grasp of gold.
The taste on your lips
is not the silver rim.

The jewels you hold close
have no value, but to
you. They cannot be
stolen and then resold.
Their shape is the wave
forming and reforming
from the undertow
that runs through your heart.

The jewels you hold close
are the first cry, the last
tear, the sigh of love
and the silence of loss.
They enter the blood
unbeholden to time.

The jewels hold you close;
never leaving, for they
are what you receive,
forever enfolding.

Your soul's shoreline in
quiet transformation.
Bejewelled.

Call/Response

When the wind rises,
rages and falls
and the dark howl
becomes a stillness
that folds over the day
like a cape.

When the centre
of the turning world
flickers, as a flame,
as a cradling
confirmation
in your open hands.

When your fingers
close around its light
to feel its kindling
warmth, and its shadows
play upon
the air you breathe.

When the pulse of
your heart is the
stream's rhythm
- its burbling wash
and its slow depth
of silence.

Then you will know
the call and response
that comes unbidden
of gazing at the moon,
and feeling only the sun
in the ocean of sky.

Sleep/Awake

When lids draw shut and eyes
in their flickering fall
into night's embrace
then we float at mercy
of currents turning
comets to water
turning water to canvas
of sky and horizon.

And awakening in this dream
life, sunlit and moon caressed,
time worn from first cry,
we are its pupils,
the painter and painted.
Each breath a brushstroke
of time, flaring and fading.
Eyes open, eyes shut.

If, 2023

I pushed apart
the i and f,
though they be close,
and stretched out the space
like this
i .... f
I pressed my hand in to the
gap and held it there to feel
the caress of possibilities
   that
               float
                             within
but the letters slid back
with nary a shrug nor sigh;
though we be small,
they seemed to say,
the paths you see
the doors ajar
the rivers rushing
to the sea
the if I do, if I did
if I had done
are the constellations
shimmering in our eyes,
our can is major
and can is minor.

If
in the shape
of their shadow
cast, in the flicker
of their light,
in the form
is the meaning,
in the word
is the world;
opening
and
closing.

Artificial Intelligence/It Could Be Anyone

The five had given up the ghost.
Not for want of trying, they cried
but the house now was not a host
how could they stay if it had died?

Though a frame still stood to the sky
its skeleton was not a soul
while it stood upright to the eye
in the bones a ghost whistle told

of whirl of words that rose and fell
in the rotation of the day
that carried once what hearts could tell
of life and not be cast away.

Now walls bare and windows clear
marked where the senses of the realm
had been, shadow lines, broken sphere
rhythm of the saints overwhelmed.

Now the earth was flat, its orbit
in the silence of gathered gloam
beyond return, senses split
from what held them together: home.

An Afternoon Storm
In the New Year

Lightning cracked
the sky
sending shards
spinning
like splinters
of wood
from an axe
singing.

Thunder poured
its growl
snapped hard
its jaws
bent the air
to say
we are not
your laws.

Hand and Glove

The hand gives life to the glove.
The form is given reason
to move with love or loss
to gather in each season.

The glove is unseen as the toll
of bell from hammer given
is not visible but heard
and so through the air is riven

to fall upon the skin and heart
the space between trough and crest
the suspended note held
from cradle to graveyard rest.

To the silence unravelling
the glove's threads then break away
and the hand becomes bone
its touch still felt down the days.

The October Poem

You open the atlas and run your fingers
along the edges of continents,
climb mountains, trace valleys,
pause at coastlines of sand and wave.

This is where you have been and this,
fingers arched, is where you want to go.
Death is too faint to be seen. Though
you know it's there, the undiscovered country,

but it is not yet borne in ink or a mark in your bones.
It is a gesture in the wings, a whisper
in your ear: I exist, and one day
we will meet. I will enter your house.

Death has passed by of course at one, two
three remove and you have watched it
through the windows or while at the door,
half in light or shade from the garden,

Or you have heard it brushing against
the roof, rustling in the trees.
But it never sat with you at the kitchen table,
offered to make a cup of tea, said you shouldn't feel

So unfamiliar with it, take heart with this if you can,
"I visit all houses, sit at all tables, will greet
your friends, neighbours, colleagues. It's no big deal to me.
And then I leave a bit of me with all of you.

"Say what you will, but I'm fair to a fault.
Emily the poet wrote of me and I was flattered:
Because I could not stop for Death —
He kindly stopped for me…"

And then, one day, death stopped at your house.
It didn't knock, but came in and sat at your table,
rubbed against your heart and then left but for
a part of itself now etched within you.

And as death left, it nodded towards
your atlas, and pointed to the contours and
shades of your world, and in the silence
of its parting, in the howling gales,

In the untouchable void you felt its wake
behind your eyes – the white-capped sea.
and you held onto this: love once lived
has no frontiers. This is your atlas.

It is October. This is the October poem.

Span

To horizon's span I reached
out my arms and gathered
in the line of sea and sky,
held it close, said not a word.

Of sun and moon a silence
deep as the tide on the rim
of the flickering blue world
rose within as wordless hymn.

This is the capture of time
we all carry from first cry
to grave: love distant is close
the light flows in sea and sky.

Stone and Star

A grain of sand in the palm
carries the universe within it,
windblown, wave washed,
its fate is to be seen but as
a speck of nothingness.

A sliver of star in the hand
carries the universe within it,
night worn and flickering,
its fate is to be seen but as
a pulse of distant light.

The arc of moon in a cracked
cup; the tapping of a philosopher's
pen on an empty page;
echo of footsteps walking away,
walking towards the held breath.

This is the world within the world.
the word within the turning word.
This is the howl and the whisper
of the wind come to rest in your palm,
saying, listen to the stone and star.

The Air Moves

When the string is touched
and the air moves,
this is love unbound.

This is the song eternal,
the rhythm constant
to sing of grace newly found

In each ebb and flow
that washes from eyes
to the open heart

Where a silence like a pool
deep and mysterious
holds your voice: to love I start

When the air is touched
and the string moves,
this is life unbound.

The Glass

The glass that is not full,
half or drop upon drop
is but mere wisp and form of thought
- the waiting and departed.

It is a silence only broken
when rim or side is tapped
and its music rises or returns
in trembling wave over wave.

And softly falling into itself
is stronger and deeper,
rubbing against the surface
it rings out, my name is love.

True North

The compass is a useful metaphor
in the directions that one takes.
Its needle is true to self when
push and pull of life forsakes

all points on the circumference rim
known by touch of hands and eyes.
Though it spins and trembles its
centre holds to light of sea and skies

that pours in day and night upon the skin
and shapes the words upon the tongue
that speak of paths and shadows cast,
of journeys false and hope still sung.

Says then the needle to the heart,
in each storm that rises to crease the air
I am you and you are me, true north
transcending, this is our whispering prayer.

The Centre of Zero

He walked along the faint-lit hall
Pondering each slow footfall:
Was there meaning in the day,
In these soft steps, in this sway?

He paused then for a moment brief
(the length of a dropping leaf)
to ask if shadow and flame
were both halves of the one frame

that shaped as it played upon the air.
It was the match and flare
came the soul's reply, the spark
and the glint, the folding dark.

He stopped, and then closed his eyes,
saw zero as sea and skies,
held close time's flickering chains
felt the heart beat in his veins.

AFTERWORD

It takes a storm to see
the rock beneath the sand,
to feel no more the grains
run through your hand.

It takes an ocean to hold
what has been washed away.
Let the waves carry love,
for love is the heartbeat's sway.

www.ingramcontent.com/pod-product-compliance
Lightning Source LLC
Chambersburg PA
CBHW042226160426
42811CB00117B/1020